ISBN 978-1-334-39166-8
PIBN 10767607

1 MONTH OF
FREE
READING

at
www.ForgottenBooks.com

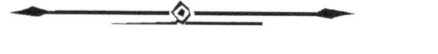

By purchasing this book you are eligible for one month membership to ForgottenBooks.com, giving you unlimited access to our entire collection of over 700,000 titles via our web site and mobile apps.

To claim your free month visit:

THE
Prefent State
OF
JACOBITISM
IN
ENGLAND.

A Second PART.

In ANSWER to the FIRST.

LONDON: Printed in the Year. MDCCII.

THE
Prefent State
OF
JACOBITISM
IN
England, &c.

That the *Paſt* and *Preſent* State of *Jacobiſm* in *England*, was and is a State of Vexation and Trouble, Suffering and Affliction, is ſenſibly felt by all thoſe who ſuſtain that Denomination, notoriouſly evident to the whole Nation, and own'd in particular by this Author, and ſome others, who make that Conſideration one Argument to induce them to take the Oaths, that thereby they may exempt themſelves from that Suffering Condition under which they have lain for ſo many Years.

In this Caſe, no Man nor Party of Men, need any Eloquence to perſuade the World, that they Act with the great-

eſt

eft clearnefs and Sincerity, if they are heartily defirous to have their Sufferings commiferated, their Burdens lightned, the Rigors againft them moderated and qualified ; For al-tho' we are taught in the School of Religion, that Afflicti-ons have their Benefit, that Adverfity, if rightly ufed, may turn to better Account than Profperity ; altho' the Doctrine of Providence obliges us to fubmit with Patience, Gon-tentednefs and Cheerfulnefs. Altho' they are always juft on God's part, always permitted or inflicted for wife and good Ends, and which therefore fhould infpire us with Hu-mility and Meeknefs, with Repentance towards God, with Charity and Forgivenefs towards Men ; neverthelefs Suffer-ings not being natural, but accidental to Religion, intro-duc'd from the Corruption of Humane Nature, by way of Difcipline and Correction, We are allow'd by the Divine Goodnefs, and in fome meafure are bound (with fit Reftri-ctions and Limitations) to pray for a removal of them from God's hand, and from any others who may be inftrumental either to our Afflictions, or Relief, and if we can find any Alleviation and Abatement, We have a new Opportunity of exercifing another Act of Religion, of praifing God, and being thankful to Men.

If therefore any Charitable hand, will either help us to mend our Circumftances, or contribute to afford us fuch degrees of Eafe and Quiet, as we may wear out the Re-mainder of our days, under the Burden only of Primative Calamities, in being depriv'd of thofe Comforts and Sup-ports, which We heretofore did, and others do now enjoy, without the Addition and Augmentation of pofitive ones. We fhall think our felves highly oblig'd both to pray for them, and alfo to make the beft Expreffions of Gratitude We are able, fuitable to the meafures of Tendernefs exer-cifed towards us : And even without any of thefe We hope we fhall never be wanting to exercife that Chriftian Duty of Charity, as to pray for them; that God will always afford
them

them that Mercy and Compaffion, which we want our felves, and cannot obtain from them.

This Author indeed tells us, that his Pamphlet *contains a* Pref *kind Invitation* to Us, and if it does, it ought to be as kindly receiv'd by us; But if inftead of an *Invitation*, it be only a Summons to furrender by a time perfix'd, or elfe to expect Military Execution, 'tis a *Kindnefs* with the utmoft degree of unkindnefs in the Belly of it ; If a Friend of our Author's fhould invite him to his Houfe, and tell him he fhould be very welcom ; but tell him withal, that if he did not come, he would certainly cut his Throat, or (which is all one) would inftigate others to do it, who were more able. I fuppofe our Author would think the *kind Invitation* a little roughly manag'd, and would defire him hereafter to keep his Kindnefs to himfelf. This is the very Cafe, For he adds in the fame Preface. *If they fhall make an ill ufe of it,* that is, if they do not forthwith what he advifes, *then they will be more inexcufable, and the Nation will be blamelefs, if a Law fhall ever be promoted to exclude them abfolutely from the Benefit or Protection of the Government ;* That is, if they are totally divefted of all the Rights and Liberties of *Englifhmen,* made Outlaws for ever , and expos'd to be knock'd on the Head, by every man who hath a mind to it. This is an Invitation after the Method of *France* ; the *French* King kindly invited his Proteftant Subjects to become Profelytes, and order'd the writing of feveral Books to perfwade them ; but when they declin'd Compliance, he back'd his Invitation with *Dragoons* and the *Gally's.*

A man had need be very fure of his Reafons, and of the Sincerity of his Kindnefs too, who makes the confequence of Refufal fo terrible. And I am confident that nothing in the World can juftify fuch meafures of Proceeding, but the plaineft Proofs and cleareft Evidence of Truth and Reafon, the higheft Wifdom and Judgment in managing them, together with a hearty and upright Regard to the Welfare of

the

the Perſons concern'd, and where any of theſe are wanting, the Propoſal is all over bloody, and an implacable Thirſt after the Deſtruction of other Men. Almighty God indeed com, mands Men to accept of His Invitations upon pain of Death, but then as we are abſolutely his, ſo His infinite Goodneſs and Wiſdom warrant the Severity of His Cominations ; His Omniſcience diſcerns all the degrees of Stubborneſs and Contumacy ; and yet after all, after manifold Tryals of Lenity and Forbearance, he ſmites only the abſolutely incorrigible. But for daring Mortals, who have neither Wiſdom to ſee their own Errors, nor thoſe of other Men, much leſs to diſtinguiſh between Miſtake and Malice, to ſet up a few weak and trifling Reaſons, and then command all Men to ſubmit to them upon pain of Deſtruction, argues equal Arrogance towards God, as Cruelty towards Men.

Why ſhould this Author be ſo conceited of his own Reaſons, as to think that the not being convinc'd by them, argues the utmoſt degree of Incorrigibleneſs ? Or if he thought ſo well of them himſelf, Why ſhould he think that we muſt do ſo too? And if they are not as Clear and Convictive to us, as (perhaps) he thinks they are to him, 'tis impoſſible that, upon that Account, we ſhould be left *inexcuſable.* Men Reaſon different ways, and ſee things by different Lights, according to differing Methods of Education, Studies, and even Temper and Conſtitution, and 'tis a Monſtrous Diſproportion of Puniſhment, that we muſt be Undone and Periſh, becauſe we have not Heads of the ſame make with the Author. He pretends indeed, to Reaſon with us upon our own Principles, but then either he does not know them, and that in him is culpable Ignorance, or he conceals them, and that is more culpable Hypocriſie.

Is it not enough, that we have bore the Burthen of Calamity for Thirteen Years together? Will no Time nor Sufferings aſſwage that Bitterneſs of Spirit? But that it
ſtill

ftill purfues us through a long Series of Adverfity, even to a Period of final Deftruction, and Extirpating of us Root and Branch? 'Tis matter of Wonder and Aftonifhment, that there are Men, who call themfelves Chriftians, the followers of the Merciful *Jefus*, who after the feveral Stages of Affliction that their Brethren have Travelled in, are ftill, for the very fame thing, calling out for new Methods of Vengeance, and irritating the Government to accumulate Sorrow upon Sorrow, to add one Weight to another, till they are Prefs'd to Death.

Poverty and Meanefs, which is a Safeguard to all Men elfe, muft, it feems, be no Security to us; we hoped that when we had parted with all for our Confciences, we had ftood out of the way of Envy, Innocence guarded with Indigence, is doubly Fortify'd. We have feen mighty Offenders, who, by quitting their Pofts, have Satisfy'd the Cries of Juftice, and they permitted to Enjoy the Spoils, without Reproof, and without Moleftation. But our withdrawing muft ftop no Profecution, and altho' it hath left us nothing, yet that Nothing muft be as keenly purfued as if we had the Wealth of the Nation to Account for, our very Rags are Criminal, and when we are Stript to the Skin, our Nakednefs muft be Scourg'd, and like Weather Glaffes, the Lower we fall, the Higher the Storms arife.

This Author tells us, *'Tis hoped none will be fo weak as to fuppofe it* (his Inviting Pamphlet) *proceeds from any Apprehenfion of their Party, or Intereft in the World.* And he is much in the right, neither he, nor any other are fo weak as to be Apprehenfive of our Party or Intereft. But then, What makes them fo free with their Threatnings? What makes them perpetually inftigating the Powers of the Land to load us with New and more Dreadful Preffures? Is it a Reafon to be Disfranchis'd, to make our very Beings Criminal, and Penal, and to lay us under the utmoft Terrors

of

of Law: becauſe no Body is ſo weak as to be Apprehenſive of Us or our Intereſt? All Mankind are agreed, that nothing can warrant the Extremeſt Rigors and Severities, but as Extreme Neceſſity ; and Penal Laws, eſpecially of a high Nature, were always forc'd from Wiſe and Good Governments, but never their Choice. But our Author puts this out of the Caſe ; For if he hopes no Body will be ſo weak as to be Apprehenſive of Us, 'tis plain that he himſelf is not ſo weak ; And yet, at the ſame time, turns us over to the moſt Diſmal Penalties he can think on : 'Tis not neceſſary (by his own Confeſſion) that we ſhould be Deſtroy'd, but we muſt be Deſtroy'd however. If this be not, What is it to be Cruel for Cruelty's ſake ? To ſubject us to the moſt rigorous Severities, not only without abſolute Neceſſity, but for no end in the World ; Neither God, nor Good Men, nor Good Laws, did ever Puniſh for the ſake of Puniſhment. And if there be no Neceſſity, 'tis mere Wantonneſs ; and at length our Author's diſtinguiſhing Kindneſs ends in this, that, like ſome of the primitive Chriſtians, we muſt be expos'd to the Lions, merely for Sport.

He further tells us, *That had we liv'd under the Deſpotick Government of* Lewis XIV. *we ſhould have found before now, if we had been ſo fond of our old Maſter, we ſhould have gone to him, there would have been no living for us. We would have had a time ſet, to comply or depart the Kingdom, we would have had no Benefit of the Law to recover our Right, but have been oblig'd to do every man Right, and bear every Wrong.* Theſe are indeed ſevere things in themſelves, and no doubt would be ſo in *France* or any where elſe. But it ſeems they are the very ſame that our Author hath provided for us here in *England,* We need not croſs the Seas, to ſave that labour, he hath tranſplanted them into our own Soil ; for all theſe frightful Cruelties expatiated on with ſo much Rhetorick, are but his own Terms in other Words,

Words, and this is only a *French* Paraphrafe of his own *Englifh* Propofal. *The Nation will be blamelefs, if a Law fhall ever be promoted to exclude them abfolutely from either the Benefit, or Protection of the Government.* That is in the French Dialect. *We fhould have no Benefit of the Law to recover our Right, but be oblig'd to do every man right, and bear every Wrong.* And that is again in *plain Englifh*: To be excluded abfolutely from either the Benefit, or Protection of the Government. Now if this be the Cafe, what is the difference between a Defpotick Government, and a Government founded upon Law? What is the difference between an Arbitrary and Cruel Adminiftration, and a mild and merciful One? If in each Government the Treatment of Perfons under their Power muft be the very fame to all Intents and Purpofes? If Men in the fame Circumftances, and for the fame Reafons muft equally *be put out of the Protection of the Law, muft have no Right, and bear all Wrong.* In vain do we talk of *Englifh Liberties*; if we muft go to *France* for Prefidents of Penalties, and take Patterns for Irritation from the moft arbitrary Government in Chriftendom. I take it for granted that our Author's flourifh upon *Lewis* XIV. was never defign'd as a Panegyrick on the goodnefs of his Government; but it is the Copy he hath fet himfelf, and he would have it exercis'd upon us. This fure is no inviting Character to recommend his Propofal to *Englifhmen*; And the fanguinary Methods of *France* are no fuch tempting Things to invite our Nation to tranfcribe from them. And he will have much to do to perfwade them, that what is Savage and Barbarous in a Papift, fo foon as it is tranflated into Proteftant hands, immediately commences Mildnefs, Good Nature, and extraordinary Charity.

The Nature and Conftitution of the *Englifh* Government is quite of another Temper, there is no room for

furious

furious and arbitrary Will to ravage and depopulate at pleasure, but the exercises of Authority are confin'd within the Bounds of Law, and those very mild and merciful Laws too, and, next to the Laws of God, there are none in the World more compassionate than our own; They will not suffer a *Butcher* to be a Juryman in Cases of Life and Death, left his Trade in Blood should harden his Constitution, wear out the Compassion of an *Englishman*, and warp him towards Cruelty. But the Equity of them never appears more than in proportioning Punishments, not only to the Nature and Quality of the Offence, but to the Condition and Circumstances of the Offender. This

Chap. 14. is the express Provision of *Magna Charta. A Freeman shall not be amerc'd for a small Fault, but after the quantity of the Fault, and for a great Fault after the manner thereof, saving to him his Contenement or Freehold. And a Merchant saving his Merchandize. And a Villain saving his Wainage. A Peer shall be amerc'd by his Peers, and after the quantity of his Trespass. No man of the Church shall be amerc'd after the rate of his Spiritual Benefice, but after his lay Tenement, and after the Quantity of his Trespass.* Here is Justice indeed, but exceedingly temper'd with Mercy, and the Law in assigning Punishments hath a double Aspect, one upon the Quantity of the Offence, as never to exceed that, of what Abilities soever the Offenders are, the other on the State and Capacity of the Offender, to lower and sink them to the proportion of his Abilities. The Equity of this extends to all parallel Cases: So that Predatory Punishments (in Cases not Capital) that devour a Man and his Family, and which exceed either the nature of the Crime, or the measure of Men's Abilities, seem directly repugnant to the old Standards of Justice and the fundamental Rights of *Englishmen.* Now upon this general View, We may easily estimate whether our Author's Proposal, be suitable to the Methods of our

An-

Anceftors, and to the Temper and Mildnefs of the *Eng-lifh* Conftitution: To be *Excluded ABSOLUTELY from the Benefit and Protection of Law*, is but all Punifh-ments in fhort: A compendious Summary of all poffible Severities, 'tis not only to be divefted of all Property, but of Freemen to be made Slaves, and that not to one Lord, but to every man in the Nation, to be obnoxious to all the Penalties the Law can inflict, and to all too that can be inflicted without Law, that is, 'tis as many feveral Penalties, as arbitrary Malice, or wanton Cruelty can invent. 'Tis *Ælia Lælia Crifpis*, neither Treafon, nor Murder, nor Felony, nor Mifdemeanor, nor Trefpafs, but All. Neither Fine, nor Imprifonment, nor Confifcation, nor Banifhment, nor Premunire, nor Hanging, but All. And now is there any need to ask, whether fuch a *Hydra* of Miferies [with a thoufand Heads, and every Head as many Stings] be an adequate and equal Punifhment, for no actual Attempt againft the Government or Laws, no Violation of any one Man's Rights? The Cafe in que-ftion is neither more, nor lefs than a pure and fingle Ne-gative, the not taking the Oath. This is intirely to deftroy the Ballance of Juftice, and there is no need of Scales, where every Offence is equally ponderous and comes up to the utmoft Standard. The nature of Crimes is confound-ed, and there is no diftinction between fmall and great, (that is in point of Punifhment, where efpecially there is moft need of Diftinction) Omiffions and Commiffions are in the fame Predicament, and Juftice is blind on the wrong fide, inftead of having no refpect to PERSONS, hath none to *Caufes*, but with an undiftinguifhing and unrelenting hand, promifcuoufly fcatters Vengeance upon all alike: Upon this foot let every *Englifh Man* hear the Equity of this Propofal, *That without any Compaffionate favings, without any regard to the Weight, Quantity, Manner of the Of-fence; Peers, Freemen, Merchants, Churchmen together with*

their

with their Peerage, Freeholds, Merchandize, Ecclefiaftical, and Lay Tenements muft for ever for one poor Negative, be indifcriminately fwept away with Deftruction, and expos'd to the utmoft Rigors, a Nation can inflict, or Men can bear.

If it be faid that this Negative, contains fomething Pofitive, and implyes Malice and Enmity againft the Government. I anfwer, this is their Conftruction, not ours; Why may it not imply as well tendernefs of Mind, and Confcience towards God? Or why may it not imply a difability to wind our felves out of our former Principles? Charity would think one of thefe. However the Law knows no *Conftructive* no more than it does *Accumulative* Treafons, nor Punifhes Men by Implications and Inferences, but from plain and evident matter of Fact. 'Tis hard that they will Judge of our Thoughts, but 'tis harder yet to faften an Arbitrary fenfe of them, and then to Punifh that Senfe of their own Impofing, which is to punifh not our Thoughts, but their own, nay 'tis to punifh us for their Thoughts. 'Tis certain no Man can know our Thoughts till we our felves Manifeft them by fome Overt Acts, by which, and by which only the Law judges; for altho' the Heart is the Traytor, and fo it is the Thief and the Murderer too, yet that which makes the Treafon, or Felony fall under the Cognizance of Law, and become the Object of Humane Juftice, is when the Enmity within is declar'd by *Overt Acts*, that is, not every Act, but fuch only as in the Eye of the Law, are fully, plainly and evidently declarative of it. Exorbitant Stretches, efpecially in Penal Cafes, have always been condemn'd by Men of Equity and Temper, but never more than in this Reign; which (We are told) is a Reign of Liberty, founded upon the People's Rights, and that now their Liberties, are not only preferv'd intire to them, but much enlarg'd; and an *Englifhman* who was always free, is now freer than ever before. And certainly *Freedom* and *fundamental Rights*, are not ambulatory and moveable, to ferve only to make Complaints with when
Men

Men are out of Power, or hardly ufed themfelves, but are fix'd and rivited in the Conftitution, and from thence (like Vital Spirits) are difpers'd to all parts and Branches of the Body Politick. And if there be fuch a thing as *Liberty,* 'tis certainly general and common to all, and not enclos'd by any Body, or Party of Men whatfoever.

Without looking into the Gonduct of other Nations in fuch Cafes, We have in our own Examples perhaps of as many Revolutions, as any other Kingdom in the whole World. Since the Conqueft (where our Hiftories run the cleareft) We have had many inftances of the Great Turns of State, of the Rife and Fall of feveral Parties and Interefts; And particularly in the days of King *Stephen,* *Edward* 2. the Two *Richards,* the long and bloody Contefts, between the two Houfes of *York* and *Lancafter,* and in the days of K. *Charles* 1ft. And indeed it muft be confefs'd, that upon the various ftrugglings for the Government, under differing Claims and Pretences, much *Englifh* Blood hath been fpilt, many Brave and Gallant Men deftroy'd, many Noble and Honourable Families for ever extinguifh'd. But if this be narrowly look'd into, it will appear in all the refpective Times, That this was moftly in the Field, *Flagrante Bello,* and in the Heat of Blood ; And I think I may truly fay, *only* and *peculiarly* with refpect to it. For fo foon as the Sword of War was fheathed, whatever Party had the better, thofe few Attainders that were made afterwards deliberately and by Law, were only of Military Men, who actually fought with, and oppos'd with their Lives and Fortunes the Claims and Pretences of the Prevailing Party, and not the thoufandth part of them neither, and much lefs of any others. And of this, befides feveral others, We have a mighty Inftance in the Reign of *Henry* 4th. which was a Reign of Pardons, and particularly the Generous Pardon he gave to Bifhop *Merks,* after his Tryal and Condemnation at the

Old-Baily, who had so openly and freely oppos'd him, and his Claim in Parliament. And I believe there is not one single Instance in all our Histories, under all the various Concuffions of State, that the Storms of the refpective Revolutions ever fell upon one single Man, who had not been in Arms, however he might, in Opinion and Judgment, be thought a Favourer of the other side. And even thefe Severities, were thought by *Henry* the 7th and his *Parliament*, fo harfh and cruel, fo contrary to Reafon and Humanity, *againft all Laws, Reafon and good Confcience*, as the Act expreffes it, That they did all that Men and Law could do, to put a final End to it, That fuch Proceedings and Practifes might never more be feen in the *Englifh* Nation. This is that famous Statute (11 *Hen.* 7. *Ch.* 1.) which exprefly provides, *That from henceforth no manner of Perfon or Perfons that attend* (the King for the time being in his Wars, or act by Commiffion from Him) *be in no wife Convict or Attaint of High Treafon, ne of other Offences for that Caufe by Act of Parliament, or by any Procefs of Law, whereby any of them fhall forfeit Life, Lands, Tenements, Rents, Poffeffions, Hereditaments, Goods, Catals, or any other Things, but be utterly difcharg'd of any Vexation, Trouble or Lofs. And if any Act or Acts, or other Procefs of Law hereafter happen to be made contrary to this Ordinance, that then that Act or Acts, or other Procefs of Law whatfoever ftand and be utterly void.* This is certainly the utmoft Provifion of Law, and 'tis impoffible that any ftronger can be made by Men. And whatever other Conftruction may be made of this Statute, 'tis evident that hereby all violent Exceffes of Revolutions are not only reftrain'd, but perfectly taken away, that however it may happen in the Field and in the Heat of War, yet that no after Ravages fhould be committed, and Men fhould not be deftroy'd by Law, who had efcaped the Sword. I need not reflect how fuitable this Law is to the mutable Eftate

of

of Mankind, and the Viciſſitudes that conſtantly accompany all Humane Affairs; And that the contrary Practiſe in the foregoing Revolutions, was nothing elſe but a Seed-plot of Deſtruction, making Sorrowful Precedents of Revenge, which, upon every turn of State, was ſure to be follow'd Home, and retalliated with Intereſt. But, it is very remarkable, that when K. *Henry* was the Regnant Power, and in Poſſeſſion of the Laws, inſtead of ſharpning the Edge of the Laws in being, or contriving new ones to Impeach, or Detect his Adverſaries, he ſhould take the direct contrary Courſe, and provide by the ſtrongeſt Law he could make, that none of his own Followers, and Adherents ſhou'd be Impeach'd, or ſuffer by any Courſe of Law, for aſſiſting him: And, the Circumſtance of Time makes this yet more Remarkable. When the Dutcheſs of *Burgundy* (an Implacable Enemy to him, and his Family) was from Abroad, ſetting on foot all poſſible ways to diſturb his Peace, when there were Spurious and Suppoſititious Titles ſet up againſt him, and, when he knew the Favourers of the other Houſe at Home were neither few, nor Inconſiderable, in this very Juncture, and in the flagrancy of *Perkin Warbeck*'s Pretenſions, and Motions, inſtead of ſending a Scrutiny throughout the Land, inſtead of framing Teſts to diſcover Mens Intentions, and try how they ſtood affected; he takes eſpecial Care to put an Everlaſting Period to the Bloody Methods of former Revolutions, and that his Followers might be Indemnified from all Attainders, Convictions, or Forfeitures for adhering to him, and Serving him in his Wars. This Wiſe King, (and a Wiſer perhaps never ſat on the *Engliſh* Throne) no doubt, did what he eſteem'd beſt for his own Security, and he thought this Method tended more to his Eſtabliſhment, than all the Sanguinary Proceedings, and Inquiſitions in the World. And, his Wiſdom did not fail him in this, no more than it had done in other great

Inſtances

Inftances, for, hereby he became an eafy Mafter of his
Enemies, Reign'd glorioufly himfelf, and tranfmitted a
clear and unconteſted Crown to his Pofterity, and who
reign'd for the moſt part in Peace, and without any confi-
derable Interruption for five Generations, till in the Reign
of the Sixth there arofe a Sort of Men, whom neither this
Law, nor the Law of God, nor all Obligations Divine
and Humane could hold from laying violent hands on, not
only the Followers and Adherents, but the facred Perfon
of the King Himſelf.

And this is the next Period of Revolutions in this Nation, and which indeed was of a Dire Complexion, more
Tragick and ghaftly than any that went before, and yet
more mild and merciful, than our Author's kind Propofal.
The Reign of the Covenant was Fierce and Cruel, turn'd
out all that wou'd not fwallow it; but then there it left
them, its Rage was fatisfy'd with their Places and Prefer-
ments, without further Purfuit of their Perfons, *An
Englishman* might be a *Non-Covenanter*, and yet an *Englishman ftill*, the Laws were as open, all other Priviledges
as free to him, as to the moſt Zealous Covenanters; And
fo foon as he was thruft out of his Office, he knew and
felt the worft of it. And altho' the Military Executions
were very bloody and Cruel, altho' the Violences upon
particular Men were very Inhumane and Bruitifh, altho'
the Compofitions for Delinquency (the then ftile of Loyalty)
were very exorbitant, yet all this notwithſtanding there
is nothing during that whole Interval of Perfidy and Treafon, of Fury and Violence, that can match the Dimenfions
of our Author. For even in the heat of War their Se-
queftrations had Savings, and there was a Refervation of
a fifth Part of the Eftate for the Maintenance of the Wife
and Children; And afterwards when they became Mafters
of the Field, and of the whole Kingdom, they forc'd the
Royaliſts, who had bore Arms againſt them to hard Compofitions,

positions, and at length disabled them from holding any Office of Truft, and from giving their Voices for Election of any Person into such Office, which, tho' very hard and unequal, tho' it was a very Intemperate and Unchristian use of their Prosperity, was notwithstanding far more moderate than the Treatment our Author prescribes, for when they had pass'd their Compositions, the Remainder of their Estates, and themselves were free, and a disability to bear Office or chuse Officers, did not disable them from any other Benefit or Protection of the Law, but bating these particular Exceptions and Limitations, all other Advantages of the Law were left open and intire to them. This was the Case during the whole Reign of the *Covenant* and *Directory*, These Men had forc'd themselves into the Possession of the Laws, and the intire Power of the Nation, they had their Adversaries in their hands, and intirely at their Disposal, they knew their Sentiments and Opinions, their steddy and immoveable Loyalty, had felt the Force of their Arms in that Cause. Yet in these Circumstances these Men (not the most merciful in the World) thought something else became them than to annihilate their Adversaries; and root out their Name and Memory from the face of the Land. The Conclusion from hence is, That if their Mercies were cruel (as indeed they were) yet in comparison of our Author's, they are Mercies indeed, and must be so accounted.

'Tis true, when they had arriv'd to the highest pitch of Villany, when they had murder'd the King, and harden'd themselves with Royal Blood, then, and not till then, they came up to the size of our Author; for then an *Engagement* was fram'd, with our Author's own Penalty upon the refusal to subscribe it, and 'tis probable he transcrib'd it from thence; for there is no other Instance of any such Proceeding, or any thing like it, throughout the whole *English* Hiftory. But this sure is no Inviting

Pre-

Precedent ; the unparallell'd Impiety of that Act, will surely reflect everlasting Infamy on the Persons and Example of the Actors ; and let it for ever be remember'd, that the Authors of the *Engagement*, and of the Act for the Tryal and Murder of *K. Charles* the First, were the same Persons; and then let every *Englishman* try his Constitution, whether it be fit to write after the Copy of the most Bloody and Barbarous Sett of Men that ever yet appear'd on the *English Stage*. And yet even this will admit of Mitigation and Abatement ; For how terrible and severe soever it was in the Enacting, yet the Execution, either never at all; or very rarely came up to it. The *Presbyterians* cry'd loudly against it, both wrote and preach'd against it, with all the Earnestness and Violence they were able, and doom'd the *Subscribers* to the Pit of Hell ; and yet as far as ever I could find, not one of them (nor perhaps any other) ever smarted under the Penalty of it.

Whitlocks Mem. p. 428.

However, upon the next Turn, when *Oliver* got the Reins in his hands, he totally abolish'd the *Engagement*, with all its hideous Train of Disabilities and Incapacities, and restor'd the Course of the Law indifferently to all Men; And the Preamble of this *Ordinaance* is remarkable ; *Whereas many General and Promissory Oaths and Engagements in former Times impos'd upon the People of this Nation, have prov'd Burthens and Snares to tender Consciences, and yet have been enacted, under several Penalties, Forfeitures and Losses ; upon Consideration whereof, and out of a Tenderness of requiring such Obligations*, &c. And this he prov'd true to all his time, and this Ordinance was confirm'd 3 Years after by his Parliament. He knew the Persons and Tempers of the Royal Party as well, perhaps better than any man in the Nation ; He knew their Principles, and Vertues, their steddy and unalterable Loyalty; He knew further they were irreconcilable Enemies to him and his

Scob. Collect. pt. 2 pag. 277.

Govern-

Government; and yet notwithstanding during his whole time, there were no *Infnaring Oaths*, nor *hampering Tests* generally impos'd. And if this was done out of *Tender-nefs,* as he pretended, it had fo far a Shew of Piety, as not to be instrumental to the prophaning and dishonour-ing the Name of God, by dreadful Menaces and Terrors to compel Men to forfwear themfelves; however, let it be for what End it would; let it be Magnanimity, Gene-rofity, Policy, or any thing elfe, it was certainly better for them, and probably for himfelf too, that when he had them in his Power, he did not provoke them for the faving their Carcaffes to damn their Souls by Perju-ry and Hypocrifie; nor yet to make their Refufal an in-humane Opportunity to revenge or enrich himfelf: He knew, as well as any man, how to dive into their moft fecret Contrivances and Councils, but his Methods for this were not by fetting on foot, (nay he perfectly laid afide) a State Engine to rip up Men's Confciences, and make their inmoft Thoughts the Objects of Punifhment. The Act that was fram'd for the Security of his Perfon, and at that very time, when there were actual Endeavours both at home and abroad to unfettle him, as both the Hiftories of thefe Times, and the Preamble of the Act it felf ex-preffeth it *as well in foreign Parts beyond the Seas, as al-fo within this Nation*; Yet the Security that he and his Parliament provided, was only againft actual At-tempts and Overt Acts; *Shall attempt, compafs, or imagine the Death*; *and fuch Attempting, Compaffing, or Imagining, fhall declare by open Deed, or fhall levy War, or Plot, Con-trive, or Endeavour to ftir up, and fhall by open Deed delare fuch Endeavour.* This was all the Security he had, and (as far as appears) all that he requir'd, and the reft he left to his own Vigilance and Care ; He knew by Ex-perience, that forc'd Oaths were no Support of any Go-vernment in the world, it might enfnare their Confciences,

but

but would prove no Security to him; Men's Fidelity arises
from the Sense of their Duty, and where that is, an Oath
is needless; where that is not, the Oath will always be
esteem'd rash or sinful, and consequently, not obligatory,
it may involve them in guilt, but can never bind them.
And therefore he quitted this Method either as fruitless or
noxious; there were no such things generally impos'd on
the Nation during his Government, and as far as I can
find all the Pubick Oaths were His to the Commonwealth,
and the Members of his Parliament to him: and consequently that no man suffer'd as a *Non-Juror* in his time;
and I may add none out of mere Disaffection or Enmity,
to him, but only for actual attempting against him; He
kept up indeed their Disability for Places of Trust, but
for other Advantages of Law, they were free to all, and
no man excluded.

But there is one thing in his Reign, that I ought not
to omit, which looks like Compassion and good Nature,
but from what Root soever it sprang, it deserves to be
taken Notice of; There were no Men in the World next
to the King, and the Royal Family, that he hated more
than the Orthodox Clergy of the Church of *England,* and
he could not do otherwise, for their Principles were directly and irreconcileably oppolite to him and his Government, and no Application could ever procure from him a
Toleration for them, as he had granted to all other Pro-
testants, of all Denominations. And in pursuance of this,
he makes an Act to eject them from their Livings; and
to be sure to have it done effectually, a Sett of Commif-
sioners are appointed in every County, and impower'd to
displace them; But then the Act contains this Proviso,
That in Case the Minister so displac'd, hath no other Tem-
poral Estate sufficient to maintain his Wife and Children;
then the said Commissioners shall allow unto the Wife and
Children of such Minister, so ejected, for their Maintenance,

icob. Coll.
t. 2. pag.
144

a

a Proportion not exceeding the fifth Part of the Profits of such Benefice, and which the Commissioners are authoriz'd to cause to be paid; and in default from time to time to sequester the Profits for the Payment thereof, and all Charges in and about the same, during the Life of the ejected Minister. And this was not a sudden Transport of good Nature, no such hasty Blast of Favour as immediately to cool, but a settl'd Resolution; For two Years after, this Ordinance was not only confirm'd by his Parliament; but a new Act was made, and which seems to be somewhat more advantageous to the depriv'd, *viz.* If the *ejected Minister have not of real Estate* 30 *l.* per Annum, or 500 *l.* of Personal Estate, then he is to be allow'd a Fifth Part during Life. So that it seems the Doctrine of *Absolute Exclusion* was a little too rigid for the hard Heart of *Cromwell* himself; He mortally hated the Loyal and Orthodox Clergy; he knew they never did, never could own him; and he depriv'd them indeed and turn'd them out, but then not only left them the Protection of the Law, but provided out of their Benefices a Proportion for their Subsistence.

To close up this, I crave leave to add a pertinent Story. When *Bradshaw* sat Judge at *Chester*, there came before him a Cause of *Meum* and *Tuum*, between a Creature of the Government and a Royalist; a mercenary Lawyer, thinking to prejudice the Royalist's Cause, begins to fall foul upon his Person, to represent him as a Delinquent and Malignant, an Enemy to the State and present Government, and one who had been in Arms for the late King. But *Bradshaw* soon stopt his Mouth, and upon that made a solemn Speech to the Auditory, importing how indecent it was to fall upon the Afflicted, how harsh and unseasonable to revive and bring into Men's Minds the Miseries of the late Troubles; That the Case before him was not Matter of State, but private Property; that he sat there not to judge of Men's Persons, or

private

private Opinions, but Caufes ; and that , .. p.r; , he
would endeavour to his Power to adminn.. J. ice e-
qually and indifferently to all Perfons. This i ... l from
one of the Auditors : And if our Author pleafe, let him
review his kind Propofal, and fee how he likes it, when
it falls fo far fhort of the Temper of the moft infolent and
bloody Regicide, that ever this, or perhaps any other
Nation, hath bred.

Upon this fhort View of the Revolutions in our own
Nation, 'tis eafie to fee how much fome Men are miftaken in their Politicks, as well as Humanity, when they
are fo frequently crying out, If you do not own the
Government, you ought to have no Protection ; if you
do not Swear, you are Inexcufable, and ought to be abfolutely Excluded from the Benefit of the Law ; if fome
Men had the handling of Thunder, the World would
quickly be made thinner ; but, Governours, as they are in
high Pofts, fo they are high in Wifdom, and manage their
Affairs, not by Paffion, and little Sentiments, but by
exact Meafures, they know, that Lenity and Forbearance
tend more to their Eftablifhment, than Rigid, and Au-
ftere Methods ; and this, as 'tis always true, fo it hath
moreover an addition of Juftice, with refpect to Revolutions, in Hurricanes, and Tempefts of State ; 'tis Impoffible that all Mens Minds fhou'd be fettled, and 'tis Im-
practicable to attempt it. Governours have the Temptations
of Honour and Profit of their Side, and, if that will not
do, to be fure Force will not, which never yet gain'd any
Man's Affent, tho' poffibly, it may an outward, and Hy-
pocritical Compliance ; and, if the Government hath not
a Man's Confcience, he hath not the Man, let him Swear
never fo much ; and, if he be driven to it by Terror, and
Compulfion, he is but fo much the more imbitter'd, and
more Enabled too to act with Prejudice, And, fo long as
there are different Sentiments in a Nation, 'tis certainly
better

better for any Government, to have them ſtand diſtinguiſh'd, for then they are known, may be eaſily watch'd, and their Attempts (if any ſuch ſhould be) as eaſily fruſtrated ; but , if they are forc'd to Incorporate into the Multitude, and made capable of the Advantages of the Government, they are thereby only made capable of doing more harm, if they are diſpos'd to it, and that even by an Authority, and Intereſt, deriv'd from the Government it ſelf, Upon theſe, or perhaps better Reaſons, the foregoing Revolutions ever declin'd the drawing Men by Violence, and Racking them into Compliance ; and, the Good, and the Bad, the Gentle, and the Tyrannous, have thought it hitherto enough for their Security, to hedge in their Perſons by the Fences of Law, againſt all Attempts, and to fill all Places of Power and Truſt, with their own Adherents, and, for the reſt, to leave them at quiet if they would, or to be otherwiſe at their Peril ; and, this middle way, as 'tis moſt agreeable to Reaſon, Humanity, and Intereſt of State, ſo it hath been verified in Fact, for, 'tis the Path, that I believe, all Revolutions have walk'd in, to be ſure all our own, except one ſingle Inſtance, which, as it was never put in Execution, ſo it is an Example of Men ſo prodigiouſly Lewd, and Scandalous, ſo abominably, and above meaſure Impious, that'tis a Horrour to think of them, and much more to Imitate them : And the Tyrannies of *Nero,* or *Heliogabalus,* are more Imitable, and fit for Example.

And yet, after all, we humbly conceive, that our Caſe is more favourable than any that went before, in ſeveral Reſpects.

There is this conſiderable difference between this, and former Revolutions, That as all former Revolutions were acquir'd by the Sword, and paſſages thro' Blood, and that not only of their Adverſaries, but their Friends, ſo the Slaughter of their own Party rankled in the Minds of the

Victors

Victors, and begot Heart-Burning, and Revenge ; but in our Cafe, the Afcent to the Throne was cafie and fafe, without Bloodfhed, without Oppofition, and confequently without any provoking occafion to Exafperate, and Inflame the Paffions, here was no room for Reprifals, none for attoning, and pacifying the Ghofts of the Slain. When K. *Edward* the Fourth came to *York*, he faw the Head of his Father, and of others, his Friends, yet remaining upon the Walls, and this did fo incenfe him, that he forthwith caus'd his Prifoners, the Earl of *Devonfhire*, and three others, to be Beheaded, and their Heads placed in the room of the others, of which Action, *Habington*, p. 19. (the Author of his Life) makes this fevere, but juft Reflection. *An action too much favouring of the Ancient Heathen; the Souls of Chriftians no way requiring their Murthers to be reveng'd, or their Injuries appeas'd with fuch an Offering.*

The Principles of the Refpective Parties concern'd, either in high Pofts of Legiflation, or otherwife under the Government, feem to plead for us, and to be Advocates for Mitigation and Forbearance. And if they pleafe to confider them in their juft confequences, We prefume they will find them moving in our Favour.

There are two general Parties in the Nation, however fubdivided ;- the *Diffenters*, and the *Church Party*, The Diffenters for a whole Age, and more, have been loudly inveighing againft *Perfecuting tender Confciences*; and by Confcience, we prefume, they do not mean only their own, but other Men's alfo, when it is truly Confcience, and not pretended, nor that this was a Temporary Doctrine, calculated for Seafons and Opportunities, and fit only to be taught their Governours, when they themfelves were in a ftate of Suffering, but conftant and permanent, as fit for them to learn, when they are in Power, as when they were under the Power of others;

And

And this can only evidence the Sincerity of their Pretenfions, and fhew that it was not Clamor, but their true Judgment, when they fhall be as ready to exercife it towards others when it is in their hands, as when it was not to demand it for themfelves. Further yet by Confcience, We prefume they do not mean only a rightly inform'd Confcience, for there is no doubt that Right ought not to be Perfecuted, but fuch a Perfwafion of Mind, which muft ultimately guide a Man whether he be in the right or wrong. That is, when a Man ufes all honeft Endeavours, and his beft Skill rightly to inform himfelf; and if after this he happens to be in an Error, 'tis rather to be pitied than punifh'd. Laftly, by Confcience being perfecuted, neither they nor we mean, the Punifhment of outward Acts and Attempts, and violations of Law; but fuch a Perfwafion, altho' differing from the Sentiments of Superiors, as is withal peaceable and quiet, offends no man, difturbs no man. Upon thefe Limitations We think, We may reafonably defire from them the Benefit of their own Principle, and We muft confefs that in their private Capacities, We have met with fair and moderate Treatment from them; Nor can I think that this *Excluding Project* came out of their Quiver. And this is yet further inforc'd, if they confider that there are two Cafes, in which their Sufferings in fome meafure run parallel with our own, that is, the *Renouncing the Covenant* and the *Sacramental Teft*, the one determin'd, the other yet in being; in both thefe Cafes they heretofore did, and yet do think themfelves hardly us'd, their natural, and Native Rights violated, and yet the utmoft Severity of both thefe, were only Exclufions from Offices and Places of Truft, which we fuffer already, and are contented to fuffer. We defire no Places of Profit and Preferment, till we comply to the utmoft; In the mean time,

D

time, if the Terms of Refufal are efteem'd fuch a Hard.
fhip upon themfelves, becaufe they cannot in Confcience
comply with them ; our declining the Oath for t' e very
fame Reafon will be no Inducement to them, acting con-
fiftently with their own Sentiments, to give their helping Hand to lay far heavier Impofitions upon Us.

In the next place the *Church Party*, We humbly conceive, have yet more Reafon for Moderation and Temper ; It is not fo long fince, as either they or We can
forget, that We were One Body, mutually agreeing in,
mutually fuffering for the fame Caufe, and (as far as we
know) upon the fame Principles. And if they pleafe to
caft their Thoughts backwards, and review our Behaviour while we walk'd with them ; We believe they will find
no Reafon to fufpect our Sincerity, nothing to provoke their Hatred or ill Will, and much lefs a fevere
and hard Treatment. But this is a String we muft not
touch upon, and Modefty bids us forbear ; however, as
We have always hitherto , fo We yet crave leave to
infift upon (and We defire to do it without Provocation
or Reflection) That the Principles upon which we fuffer,
were their own, as well as ours ; And if they are fo ftill,
for them or any of them to be inftrumental in laying
on our Afflictions, is to prey upon their own Principles ;
it favours too much of the Cannibal, and is devouring
their own Kind ; and to fee *Paffive Obedience* crucifying
Paffive Obedience, is the moft unnatural thing in the
World, and which can be parallell'd by no other Party
or Perfwafion befides. And whenfoever they concur or
give their Vote for our Miferies, in Religious and Mo-
ral Conftruction, they lay violent hands on themfelves,
and commit Outrage in our Perfons, on their own Sentiments, and Thoughts of their Hearts. If it be faid
here, that We lay thefe Principles on too narrow a
. bottom,

bottom, and we ought to have underſtood them in their juſt Latitude. We anſwer : Be it ſo, why then, the Conſequence is, That the ſame Principle ſtreightned and contracted, confines the Behaviour within narrower Limits, when the ſame open'd and enlarg'd, gives greater Liberty in Practice. But 'tis a ſtrange Latitude indeed, and gives a monſtrous Turn to it, which impowers it to deſtroy and devour the ſame, though ſtreighter ; 'Tis certainly the ſame Principle, however modify'd, and if by vertue of a new Modification it can contract ſuch terrible Qualities, the mildeſt Principle in Religion may ſoon be modify'd into the moſt Savage and Bruitiſh ; 'tis but tacking a Latitude to it, and then it may do any thing in the world. However, let the Foundation be what it will, We have laid it no narrower than they have done themſelves, our Principles are in their Laws, Books, and Sermons litterally and expreſly, without any ſuch Latitude, or Caution ; and if We have ſwallow'd them implicitly, or with due and reaſonable Care, have examin'd and entertain'd them, ſome ſhare certainly of the Miſtake (if ſuch it be) is owing to them, and they, in ſome degree, are reſponſible for the natural Conſequences of their own Doctrines and Inſtructions ; And 'tis a hard way of paying of Debts, and attoning for the Inconveniences into which they have lead us, by aſſaulting us with Vengeance, and helping forward our Deſtruction. If it be yet further ſaid, that they have quitted theſe Principles upon good and ſubſtantial Reaſons, let that be granted too, then that is in the nature of Repentance ; And the natural and proper Effect is to produce Compunction and Grief, for having been miſlead themſelves, and for having been inſtrumental to ſeduce others ; but it operates the wrong way, if inſtead of begetting Sorrow in our ſelves, it ſerves only to heap

up

up Sorrow on the Heads of others. This is indeed an
Act of Revenge, but the Object is miftaken; For in
fuch Cafes, the Object of Revenge is a Man's own felf,
and there it ought to terminate, and not on his Bro-
ther, tho' he be miftaken, 'tis a mere Secular Device
and Artifice, and hath nothing at all of Religion, when
Men think to evidence the Sincerity of their Change
by falling foul on the Principles or Party they have
quitted; they may give their Reafons with the beft Advantage they can, but fure 'tis fit, that at the fame
time they with hold their Hands, for of all things Force
and Violence are moft undecent and unbecoming Qualities in a Convert. And look throughout the World,
from the Days of _Cain_ until now, and you will certainly find, That Renegado's and Apoftates only, have
been the Perfecutors of their former Brethren, and that
'tis only a Confcioufnefs of forfaking the Truth that fours
their Tempers, and degenerates into Fury. For a Re-
covery from Error upon honeft and full Conviction is
quite another thing, it always leaves upon the Soul a
ftrong Impreffion of its own Infirmity, the Experience
of their own Errors, joyn'd with the Ingenuity of own-
ing and forfaking them, infpires them with Thoughts
fuitable, and begets Candor and Mildnefs towards the
Errors of others, with a more particular Tendernefs to
the Cafe we have been involv'd in our felves; And
whatever Arguments for Compaffion may be drawn
from the lapfable Eftate of Mankind, they are tenfold
more Cogent and Weighty, if the Lapfes were once
our own; If we our felves have been overtaken in the
fame Cafe, and in the fame Inftances. So that upon
the whole, turn it which way you will, Let the _Party_
of the Church either believe the fame Principles that we
do, or let them hold them in a differing Latitude; or
let

let them perfectly forsake them (which three Divisions we believe include at least nine Parts in ten) in all respects, and with reference to all the Divisions, the thing we are Pleading against, is equally repugnant, and inconsistent, as unaccountably Harsh, and Severe.

We have a Mighty Instance in our own Nation, to Illustrate this whole matter. In the days of Queen *Mary*, we see the false Principles of the *Roman Church*, join'd with the Apostacy of those who complied in the former Reign, spread themselves all over the Nation, in Martyrdoms, and Executions, in all the Bloody, and Violent Methods that Rage and Malice could Invent, or Execute. From whence it hath been well obferv'd, That that is a strange Religion which divests Men of Humanity, which, instead of smoothing the Asperities of Humane Nature, Enhances, and Inflames them, and makes them ten times more Fierce and Cruel by Religion, than they were by Nature. But, so soon as the *Reformation* recover'd again under Queen *Elizabeth*, the Spirit of Mildness, and Mercy reviv'd with it. Fire and Faggot were at an End, and the Triumphs of Truth were seen not in Slaughters and Bloody Victims, but in Living objects of Mercy. The Queen her self had been very ill used, and withal, in great danger of her Life; the Provocations in general had been very high, and Exasperating to Flesh and Blood, the Wounds many and deep, and withal, fresh and Bleeding; and, yet behold the mighty Power of Truth, and true Principles, which, instead of pursuing Revenge Abroad, subdued the Tyranny of it within, and tied up the Hands of Power from retributing the like measure on themselves. The Reformation indeed, went on with Resolution and Courage, but it was with great Piety too, as the Case was Religion, so it was Intire, and Uniform in all its
Parts;

Parts ; Faith had not yet devour'd Good Works ; Zeal had not eaten up Charity ; the Name *Proteſtant* in thoſe Days, meant the *Thing*, a mild, and merciful Religion and which inſpir'd all its Votaries and Proſelytes with the ſame qualities. It is true, Non-Compliers were diſabled from holding any Offices, and the Clergy were actually depriv'd for refuſing the Oath of Supremacy ; but, their Deprivations were ſo Temper'd with Compaſſion, and Kindneſs, that they became not only Tolerable, but very Eaſie. In the *High Commiſſion*, the Commiſſioners

Penſiones legittimas congruasꝯ competentes cedentibus vel reſignantibus Hiſt. of Reform. pt. 2. p. 400. are expreſly Impower'd to aſſign *fit, and Competent Penſi-ons*, to thoſe who were put out, and of which, the Hiſtorian ſaith, *The Prudence of reſerving Penſions for ſuch Prieſts as were turn'd out, was much applauded.* And, if that was all, *Prudence* is a Vertue both Laudable, and imitable ; But much more where Piety is joyn'd with Prudence, and the grounds of ſuch mild Proceedings are Religious, as well as Prudential. Thus upon the indulgent Treatment of the Depriv'd Biſhops, *viz.* That *Heath* Archbiſhop of *York*; lived ſecurely at his own Houſe in *Surrey*, and was viſited by the Queen. That *Tonſtal* and *Thirleby* liv'd in *Lambeth* with *Parker*, (the New Arch-Biſhop) with great Freedom and Eaſe. That even *Bonner* himſelf (the bloodieſt of them all) was ſuffer'd to be in ſafety, and Skreen'd from the Fury of the Enrag'd Multitude. The ſame Hiſtorian makes this Reflexion : *As the Queen was of her own Nature merciful, ſo the Reformed Divines had learned in the Goſpel not to render evil for evil, nor to ſeek Revenge. And as* Nazianzen *had of old exhorted the Orthodox, when they had got an Emperor that favour'd them, not to retaliate on the* Arians *their former Cruelties, ſo they thought it was for the Honour of their Religion, to give this real Demonſtration of the Conformity of their Doctrine to the Rules of the Goſpel, and of the*
Primi-

Primitive Church, by avoiding all Cruelty and Severity, when it look'd like Revenge. Now if thefe were good Doctrines then, they are certainly fo ftill, and come home to our Circumftances with all poffible Advantage, there is indeed a great Difparity between the two Cafes, but every branch of the Difparity turns in our favour, and concludes in all refpects more ftrongly for us. We need not purfue the Comparifon, a Man that Runs may Read it, both with Refpect to them, and to our felves. This Author is now in a Poft to give Evidence of his own Doctrine ; and, if the *Honour of the Reformation, the Rules of the Gofpel, and of the Primitive Church,* have any Prevalency at this Day, we may yet hope to fee the Confequences of them in Practice, the fame Celebrated Effects reviv'd a mongft us, and Demonftrated in real Acts of Clemency, and Forbearance ; and therefore, We cannot conclude better, than in the next Words of the fame Hiftorian, (which were not fpoken Exclufively, but, by way of Panegyrick, as a Noble, and Pious Example, fit for himfelf, and others to Imitate.) 𝔄𝔩𝔩 𝔱𝔥𝔦𝔰 𝔪𝔦𝔤𝔥𝔱 𝔥𝔞𝔳𝔢 𝔟𝔢𝔢𝔫 𝔈𝔵𝔭𝔢𝔠𝔱𝔢𝔡 𝔣𝔯𝔬𝔪 𝔰𝔲𝔠𝔥 𝔞 𝔔𝔲𝔢𝔢𝔫, 𝔞𝔫𝔡 𝔰𝔲𝔠𝔥 𝔅𝔦𝔰𝔥𝔬𝔭𝔰.

F I N I S.

CPSIA information can be obtained
at www.ICGtesting.com
Printed in the USA
BVHW091439211118
533722BV00030B/2578/P